Overcoming
Along The Carolina Lowcountry

Thomas J. Pyatt

ISBN: 978-0-9767079-5-0

www.tjpyatt.com

Dedication

A special dedication posthumously, to my parents, Charlie Sr. and Sarah G. Pyatt. A special tribute to Mom and Dad, with deep appreciation, and gratitude. It is often the parents who make the greatest impression on their children at a very young age. Mom and Dad provided for us from day one. They were very strong God fearing people with a deep faith and sense of self worth.

They provided sufficient food and shelter, and gave their five children a very profound upbringing with a strong foundation in God. They had such Wisdom, Knowledge and Understanding that could have only come from God. They were both compelled to go to work at a very young age due to the circumstances at that time. They had the experience of life and instilled in us what we needed to excel in this wayfaring land.

They endured and overcame many obstacles, and their struggles and sacrifices made it possible for us to enjoy the good life today. We can see it in what we have accomplished and obtained, based on the foundation they instilled in us. They made it possible for us to get a very good education and enjoy what we have today. We must never forget their history, for it is our history. We are what we are today because of their sacrifices and guidance. They did not have or enjoy some of the material things we have today. But their life was filled with a deep and abiding faith that brought them through in better shape than many people of today.

The house they built over threescore years ago still stands today, and is a memorial and living legacy to them. It was a joy growing up in that house in a community with a deep sense of caring, and with some very good neighbors.

Mom and Dad you were and are so special, a tribute is not sufficient. Our Appreciation and Gratitude is Eternal, and we thank God for letting you do what you did for us. Placing a flower is but a small token of our appreciation and deep respect. We know that we shall meet again, even beyond that great millennium. As all God's children will be with Him in that Great Eternity. Thank God for Mom and Dad.

Thomas J. Pyatt

Contents

Overcoming

Along The Carolina Lowcountry
And Beyond

Introduction

On a hot and steamy sunny summer afternoon here near the ocean at a resort by the sea, as I sit in my villa looking at the inlet and lake; with hikers and bikers on the pathways trying to enjoy one last week of summer fun before the school year starts. This is a very peaceful retreat where one can relax, pause and reflect on the hectic trials of life today with its many stresses and strains that can easily wear one down. Here by the ocean it's peaceful and tranquil, and one can clear their head here down on the Carolina Lowcountry by the Atlantic Ocean.

There's a tremendous amount of history here along this stretch of the Carolina Lowcountry, especially in some of the Gullah communities tucked away here near or on the Sea Islands. A few of the Sea Island communities are as isolated as they were a century ago. Lifestyles haven't changed much in some of those tucked away isolated communities where the culture has been passed down from generation to generation; and where the people have been OVERCOMING obstacles for centuries.

The elder generation would have get-togethers by the river under the old oak trees, and pass along stories and traditions to the younger generations. As we sat under the old oak tree at sunset listening to the elders tell their stories, the old man looked and saw his reflection in the last sunset; and he knew that the subsequent generations would have to take a long journey into deep, deep waters. The elder generation knew that a change would come; and that the next step would have

1

to be an Economic Step; and that we all might just as well Come Now!

The elders shared their wisdom there by the water's edge under those old oak trees; they could see that without a knowledge of one's history and culture that the younger generation would lead their children back into Economic Bondage. The elder generation knew that the youngsters needed the proper training in order to participate in the OVERCOMING; and with no proper training and discipline they would not be able to stand up and compete in the highly technological 21st century Global Economy. Many youngsters are seeking to do things their way, and refusing to seek job training in order to obtain an Economic Skill to be prepared to compete in this highly technological 21st century Global Economy. Our elders knew that a change would come! And for those who are prepared, An OVERCOMING!

An OVERCOMING of major obstacles will be needed in the days ahead; a Luciferian influence has permeated a large segment of the land, and a few too many institutions have become inept and dysfunctional, in the midst of too many drug infested neighborhoods throughout the land. There are also those who are there dancing with the Devil in the Devil's Den, while the den's on fire. As in the days of Noah, some people will end up on the wrong side of the flood. Our elders taught us to be strong so many decades ago. There was a lot of wisdom there by the water's edge so many decades ago. The elders understood the prophecies of old; the prophet Daniel looked and he saw the abomination of desolation standing where it ought not be.

A change will come just as it is written in the Word of God. There are no political panaceas and no secular solutions for the problems that confront the land today (II Chronicles 7:14, Deuteronomy 28:13).

Some will keep spinning wheels in the mud pile while stuck in the stupid zone. We cannot bail ourselves out by stuffing money in the holes in the dike, while remaining on the wrong side of the flood, while the river is still rising. It may be a very painful and prolonged Economic Stagnation, with many still marching off the deep end of the cliff. Our faith must remain deep and strong while we stand on a solid foundation; because a Change Will Come, An OVERCOMING! Our Elders told us about these days so many decades ago, with their many stories there under the old oak trees so many decades ago; stories such as:

Wisdom By The Water's Edge
Sunset Under The Old Oak Tree
The Old Man's Reflection in The Last Sunset
A Journey Into Deep, Deep Waters

Many other stories and traditions were passed along there in those tucked away isolated communities in the Carolina Lowcountry. In the midst of the uncertainties of these latter days our elders taught us to remain on a strong foundation, and seek Wisdom, Knowledge, and Understanding (Proverbs 1:7, 2:6, 3:5, 4:7). Most of them had little or no formal education, but they had a tremendous amount of wisdom there by the water's edge. They were informed and had a lot of information, and were very good at perceiving and comprehending; their knowledge and understanding were also God given. We learned a lot there at sunset under the old oak tree, much wisdom there by the water's edge.

The Old Oak Trees Still Stand There
Beside The Water's Edge

. Wisdom By The Water's Edge

There is an old isolated pristine island that sits along the coast of the Carolina Lowcountry, and the island has remained virtually unchanged for centuries. Many of the residents of the island today are direct descendants of the freed slaves who founded settlements on the old isolated island over a century ago. That old island is Sandy Island, and my father was born and raised there, and I spent many summers there growing up as a young child. The residents maintained their distinct culture and heritage as it was passed down from generation to generation. It is the Gullah culture as passed down by the slaves who were brought here from West Africa so many centuries ago. The island is surrounded on the east by the Waccamaw River, on the west by the Great Pee Dee River, on the north by Bull creek, and on the south by Thoroughfare Creek.

The main Gullah settlement is still there right by the water's edge of the Waccamaw River. The settlement is called Mount Arena and has traditionally been a gathering place for all the Gullah communities on the island, even though other settlements are located a couple of miles away. There by the water's edge is where the residents meet to get news and listen to the elders tell stories of life on the island so many years ago. The elders are eager to pass along what they have learned to the younger generation.

I remember stories they told me when I was visiting there during my summers as a young child over a half century ago. After so many decades I still visit the old island, and on a recent visit I took along a friend from the city. My friend

Patty asked the most senior elder why they chose to remain on this old isolated island for so many decades.

I knew that Patty would get a good answer because the most senior elder was related to me. Everyone knew his name but everyone referred to him as the old man of wisdom that lives there by the water's edge. He lives there at Mount Arena and stands on his front porch not far from the banks of the Waccamaw River and watches the sun as it sets over the horizon of the river.

Before he answered Patty, he very calmly sat down in a big chair under the old oak tree and brushed a little sweat from his forehead. Then he said, Miss Patty, young lady I am now well over fourscore years old, and I still reside near the water's edge just a few feet from the banks of that old ferocious black water river.

I still watch the sun rise and set over the mighty river just as I have for decades. But it's a little sweeter now that I am retired and isn't forced to rise way before sunrise in order to work the land for a living. In the old days I had to rise up many a day before daybreak in order to get to work on time.

I was born and raised here on this isolated old pristine island that still sits way back in time. The scenes have not changed in centuries, and the centuries old moss laden oak trees still stand tall all over the isolated island. Those old oak trees have been there for generations and have seen many generations come and go. I strolled under the old oak trees with my parents, and now I continue to stroll under the same old oak trees with my children and grandchildren. It was a hard life back then, and I went away to serve in World War

II, and came back by choice. It's still an amazing life right here by the water's edge on this old isolated pristine island, full of peace and tranquility. Miss Patty, this is my home.

Patty and I looked at each other and realized that the old man has a lot of wisdom, wisdom from experiences of life and the wisdom of the ages. We're very fortunate to have such old elders still with us to impart such wisdom that could have easily been lost or forgotten decades ago. This is a deep, deep living history and something I will never forget as I sat there listening to him continue to tell stories about the people who lived there over a century ago who had given him advice such as his parents and grandparents. I was also keenly interested in such history because it was also part of my history as my roots are also deeply embedded there on that old pristine isolated island. Each time I go to that old isolated island I still recall and reflect on the good old days and times I had visiting on the island for extended periods of time. The old big house in which the old man was born and raised still stands there ageing away on the other end of the island.

The old sandy roads leading from the old big house still are very deserted and one sometimes gets a haunting feeling walking down those old sandy roads and pathways from one settlement or village to the other on both ends of the old pristine isolated island. The old man still tells many stories of so many residents that have long died out now, and only their memories linger there now. The old man talks about the life and times of the generations long gone and how they lived and frolicked around as children under the same old moss laden oak trees. They also had some wonderful days on the mighty and ferocious black water river and on the peaceful shores of the riverbank.

Patty noticed that in the stories that the old man tells there is always the big house, the old boat dock, and coming across the mighty and ferocious black water river in a small row boat so many decades ago. The old man told us the story about how he and his cousins, Ben and Paul, were stuck on the mainland side of the river way up into the night while a very bad storm passed. It sometimes got too rough to cross the river in a small row boat during a big storm. It is still too rough to cross the river during a big storm in a small motor boat today. After a few hours the storm let up enough for them to cross the river in their small row boat. It was a dark, dark and starless, moonless night as the old man and his two cousins made their way across the river to the old boat dock that no longer exists. The old boat dock was located down the rounding bend in the river tucked back between some old moss laden oak trees.

It was so dark that night that the moss on the trees can sometimes be mistaken for the shape or form of a person. There were no electric lights on the old isolated island back then when the old man was a young man.

The old man said he was sitting in the middle of the boat paddling the boat while his cousin Paul sat at the front of the boat, and his cousin Ben sat at the back of the boat. After they crossed the river through the dark and moonless night and reached the old boat dock on the other end of the island. Ben asked his cousin Paul, who was that sitting there next to you in the front of the boat. Paul was speechless for a moment, and then he replied, there was no one sitting next to me, as we were the only three people on the boat. As the old man tells the story his cousin Ben at the back of the boat never changed his story even after decades had passed. The old man was in the middle of the boat with his back to Paul as he was paddling the boat. Sometimes in such isolation the mind sees things or images that are really not there in a physical dimension.

It was a commonly held belief that on certain dangerous nights on the river that the spirits of the islander's ancestors return to watch over them as they maneuver their way across the mighty and ferocious black water river. Many a souls have been drowned over the years in the river by all type of occurrences, such as waves from big boats, logs or other debris in the river that can easily overturn a small boat. During stormy weather one has to be especially careful because all types of debris and objects can get blown into the river from the shore.

The old man says that sometimes you can feel the presence of someone else with you as you travel over the treacherous river on dangerous trips in very bad weather. I can remember back when I spent my young summers on that old isolated island that I sometimes saw something in the distance down those sandy roads and as I got nearer it was gone. It's difficult to explain but I know that I have experienced things on that old pristine isolated island that I have experienced nowhere else. It truly is a spiritual experience being that far back in time, and other people also having similar experiences about some areas on the island that they say are kind of eerie, or makes them feel strange or not alone while in those areas. And now when I visit those areas I never go alone, as I don't want to flash back too much and start to imagine and see things that are not there.

Patty asked me whether some stories are fact or fiction, I paused and reflected and said, we may never know for sure whether it's all fact or fiction or part or all myth. But I know for a fact that I have had some very different, strange and unique experiences there where so many generations have toiled and passed on before us. The old man has spent many decades there before us and frolicked with generations before him and generations after him, and he says with confident wisdom that whatever happened was for the best. I trusted the old man's wisdom as a child growing up and I still trust the old man's wisdom today over a half century later. His wisdom is profound and deeply rooted by the water's edge way back there on that old pristine isolated island.

He has seen it all over so many generations and decades that I know that the knowledge he now imparts is pure and deeply rooted in spiritual reflections. He has seen it all and is still passing down such wisdom there by the water's edge to all, especially the youngsters. He is keenly aware of his responsibility and obligation to pass down such wisdom and insights there by the water's edge in his magnificent golden years. He still tells me to do the best you can and keep moving on and you will succeed and accomplish much in life, for you have much more resources and opportunities than your ancestors had. Just pause and reflect once in a while and you will see your vision right there before you, so just keep moving on as you see it and it will get clearer and in perspective just for you. The best advice is often received from someone who has successfully lived the experiences of life, and they are often right here among us as we look all over everywhere else for role models.

The old man told me decades ago that I should get a good education as my generation would receive more opportunities than his generation received. But that I should also seek wisdom, knowledge and understanding from a higher source. I also remember my parents telling me that I should get wisdom and with all thy getting get understanding, and that only God can give us true wisdom, knowledge and understanding. They also encouraged me to study and work to get a good education in school and beyond. It was years later as I got older that I realized that they were telling me exactly what Proverbs 4:7, 2:6 and 3:5 was saying.

I became even more convinced that their wisdom came from a higher source. The old man is the last of that generation there now by the river. Many people have learned from his wisdom that he is indeed someone special sent to us by a higher power. We don't just call him an old man anymore, or just one of our elders. We have been calling him the old man of wisdom that lives by the water's edge, not too far from the bank of that mighty and ferocious black water river. The old man of wisdom is still there imparting his knowledge and experiences of life to all who care to listen, especially youngsters.

The old man of wisdom is also the most senior elder on the island and his guidance is sought in formulating rules and procedures for the residents to follow. This is something that goes back many decades to the villages on the isolated island, as there still is no police or police department or government offices on the isolated island. The elders, especially the most senior elders in the big house laid down the law, rules and procedures that everyone should follow. The rules were all predicated on the Golden Rule, Commandments and Word of Truth. I don't even recall anyone getting out of line that required any type of law enforcement. The folk ways of the people and their community has sustained their lifestyle on that pristine old isolated island for generations from slavery unto this very day. The big house in the village was a place we always looked to being at as the sun was setting, because we knew we could have a nice big family dinner, and listen to some stories with a lot of wisdom told by the elders at the big house.

As we sat on the porch under the stars, the old man of wisdom sat in his old rocking chair and said to Patty, young lady I'll tell you the story of some of the early people on the island decades ago and some events that happened over fourscore years ago. We all had to work the land and take care of the live-stocks at a very young age. The grown-ups were up way before day break getting ready for a hard day's work. Some of the men worked on some of the old logging roads back on the back side of the island decades ago. At certain times of the day or after sunset as you frolicked back into and onto those old haunting logging roads you can sometimes feel and hear something that sounds like logging in the distance.

But as you get to the actual scene of the old logging camps you can see that they have been deserted for decades, and there's no one there. It must have been the wind a-whistling, or perhaps one was just thinking a little too hard about the time and days that people spent here on these old logging roads here way back in time on this old isolated island. There's been nothing here for decades except the old moss laden oak trees looking out over what time has deserted and forgotten. If those old moss laden oak trees could tell the stories of what they've seen over the generations and centuries we all may be better off for it.

The old man of wisdom told Patty that you can sometimes see reflections in the old moss laden oak trees along the old forgotten logging roads as you leave the area at dusk as the sun goes down into the last sunset. It sometimes appears as reflections of old loggers working away not ready to call it a day just yet. I still prefer not to journey out alone too far from the big house at night, especially on a dark, starless, moonless night as it is too easy to see what appears to be forms or reflections that are really not there? It really is the physical isolation that sometimes makes it difficult to accept the fact that you are actually the only one out there on that little piece of the old isolated island. But don't worry because everything that happens out there is for the best. Patty was very silent and was awed by what she was hearing and experiencing.

The old man of wisdom and the other elders have told stories at the big house for decades, just as they were told other stories, etc. at the big house when they were young growing up. From all the stories it is abundantly clear that the fundamental lifestyle on the old pristine isolated island remains virtually intact after so many generations and centuries of physical isolation. The settlements or villages were first settled by their ancestors during post reconstruction. They always had a very deep faith and the churches were the cornerstones of the little settlements called villages. The history of the first freedmen settling the communities during post reconstruction is very well known on that old isolated island.

It was getting late into the night but the old man of wisdom continued on to tell the story of how as a child he helped his parents work the land and care for the live-stocks, etc. They had all kinds of live-stocks they needed to be a self sustaining community in the midst of such physical isolation. They even planted their own gardens and had fruit trees, grapes, berries, and hunted wild games and went fishing in the mighty black water river. The old man of wisdom still passes on such insights and knowledge to the little children of today. Some of the youngsters asked him how did they plow the land when they worked the land, and how did they feed and care for the mule. The old man of wisdom pointed out to the youngsters that it would not have been cost effective to buy a mule to plow on the isolated island; because a mule would not have been self sufficient in such physical isolation, as they would have needed a stable and buy food for the mule.

The old man of wisdom then asked the youngsters what other animal could have been used to plow, and still be a self sufficient animal and provide food, meat, milk, etc. that the people needed to survive. The old man of wisdom pointed out to the youngsters that a cow or bull was the ideal choice to use to plow because the cow and bull had a multiple purpose and use in such isolation. It didn't cost anything to feed the cows and bulls as there was plenty of grass all over the island and water at the inlets to the river. The cows provided milk for all and fresh meat, some of which was always a-curing in the storehouse not too far from the big house.

There was complete silence as the old man of wisdom pointed out that one of the main lessons he learned many decades ago was to utilize what you have to produce what you need in your current environment under the current circumstances. He pointed out that the cow, bull or oxen were also used as a motor vehicle as there were no vehicles on the island decades ago. He told stories of how they made carts for the oxen to pull along the sandy roads, and such carts were used to carry firewood to the big house. The oxen carts were also used as a hearse for funerals on the old isolated island decades ago. The old man of wisdom pointed out that one must be creative with a vision, and use what you have to accomplish the tasks at hand. Patty looked at me and nodded her head in agreement, and I could see that she would have fitted in very well on this island.

The old man of wisdom reminded the youngsters that the same is true even today; that we must plow and plant in order to have a good harvest. This may sound somewhat strange to the youngsters of today in this highly technological 21st century society where you can just purchase what you need. But the old man of wisdom pointed out to the youngsters that first you must be able to purchase by becoming self sufficient, and acquire the economic skills that will enable you to compete in the global economy.

That this fundamental lesson to plow and plant in order to have a good harvest is from a higher source, and is still valid today; in the sweat of thy face will we till the ground all of our sojourn here (Genesis 3:19, Galatians 6:7). We still have a fundamental duty to Study and Work (I Thessalonians 4:11, II Thessalonians 3:6-12).

You could feel that the old man of wisdom was speaking from decades of experience, and he knew that his wisdom, knowledge and understanding came from a higher source that is still in effect today. He has resided so many decades on the isolated island and seen so many generations come and go, and is distinctly aware of certain distinctions in each generation. He points out that many of the younger generation tends to believe that a good education which is very essential today is all they need. He constantly reminds them that they also need to acquire wisdom, knowledge and understanding just as their ancestors did. That they should not neglect to plow and plant, have goals, objectives and a vision; Study and Work and you will have a good harvest. You will ultimately only reap what you have sown, for it is written "that every man should eat, drink and enjoy the good of all his labour, it is the gift of God" (Ecclesiastes 3:13).

The old man of wisdom then turned to Patty and said, I still sit on my front porch, and I stroll along the bank of the mighty and ferocious black water river every day. The river still flows down river to the ocean just as it has for centuries, as all the rivers flow to the sea, yet the sea is never full, as stated by the preacher in the message to the flesh man that walks under the sun. I am just a messenger delivering a message to the younger generation. The messenger's role is to deliver the message he was given to deliver; the true messenger cannot alter the message in any manner.

The old man of wisdom continues to impart many stories of the ages filled with wisdom, just as he has been doing for decades and generations. And when he leaves and is finally gone, we'll all look there by the water's edge for such wisdom of the ages, and see the old man of wisdom reflections in the last sunset as he journeys on.

Patty seemed to be reflecting on what the old man of wisdom had said, but Patty didn't say anything. As we were leaving the old isolated island crossing the Waccamaw River in our small motor boat, Patty looked back and said to me, I can still see the old man of wisdom there by the water's edge. I nodded and said he's not just my cousin and the most senior elder on the island; he is truly the old man of wisdom that lives there by the water's edge.

Tremendous wisdom was passed along there by The Water's Edge in those tucked away isolated communities down along the Carolina Lowcountry. Many generations have seen sunset there under the old oak trees.

Many Generations Have Seen Sunset
There Under The Old Oak Trees

Sunset Under The Old Oak Tree

Deep down along the coast of the Carolina Lowcountry there are many old moss laden oak trees that abound all over the land, swamps and wetlands. But there is a very special big old oak tree that sits quietly in its little country setting deep and way back in a long time country community deep in the Carolina Lowcountry. This community is the Sandy Island community, and the old moss laden oak tree is at the Sandy Island Landing on the mainland side of the island. The old oak tree sits and stands not too far from the river just as it has for centuries, with its old moss laden limbs. It looks old and tired and still looks like it is trying to seek some rest. You can even feel this even as so many people keep coming to seek rest from the hot sun, and find shade under its moss laden old limbs which still spread so majestically wide for comfort for all who come to seek its shelter and comfort. Everyone is welcome to come and enjoy a little comfort from their weary sojourns.

The old moss laden oak tree sits right in the middle of a landing by the river, and is naturally and ideally situated in a spot where people come to congregate as they move on to their daily destinations. There are a few made by the way picnic tables, and some other sit down handmade seats to accommodate the weary travelers for a little while. A few of the locals even arrange get- together there some evenings and well into the night long after the sun has gone down over that mighty black water river. It is one of the few focal points or meeting place this way back in the county community has.

19

The elders tell stories after sunset under the old oak tree as many of the locals gather there to seek their advice. A few of the locals even spend most of their days off right here under the old oak tree telling stories and reminiscing about the good old days, as many of them have been coming to this very spot for decades and have seen and experienced much over the years.

One of the local's that's there most evenings to watch the sun set under the old oak tree is an old timer everyone calls "Big Papa". He lives just across the river from the old oak tree and gets a ride across the river every day just so he can sit under the old moss laden oak tree and greet and meet everyone as they come and go on their daily journey. Big Papa is retired now and doesn't operate a motor boat anymore, and he just gets a ride across the river from someone. Big Papa was born and raised way back here in this country community deep in the Carolina Lowcountry. He moved away to some of the nearby towns and cities after graduating from high school near here so many decades ago. Now that he is retired he was drawn back by the pull of the mighty black water river, and just got off here under the old oak tree that still sits and stands right there in the middle of the landing by the river.

Big Papa has heard many stories over the years, and he patrols the area just by sitting there under the old oak tree showing his presence. He knows almost everyone who comes there or he knows their family from long ago. He speaks to everyone that comes along with an inquisitive question or comment. As I approached to take a seat under that old oak tree on a sunny afternoon, he asked me if he knew me, I told him I don't think so. He kept talking and he knew all my

20

cousins that lived on the island across the river. He also told me that he was retired now and had lived all over and asked where I lived. I told him that I lived in that old historic riverfront town called Conway, and was here to visit my cousins.

He proceeded to tell me that he once lived in Conway and had resided in the Sugar Hill neighborhood. I knew the Sugar Hill area of town pretty well as it was not too far from our little Whittemore community in Conway. So now Big Papa had a reason to keep on talking and asked me if I was a preacher. I told him not at the present time but that I always keep a sermon prepared for just about any eventuality, and why did he need to know. He opened his lunch bag and showed me that he had something to drink and that if I was a preacher he was not going to drink in front of me. I reminded him that I'm not the one he need to worry about as I'm only delivering the message. I changed the subject and told him that I could tell him a story about how I stopped the Sugar Hill Gang over a half century ago.

Sugar Hill Gang – I sat down on the bench beside Big Papa and told him that a half century ago the Sugar Hill section of Conway was separated from 9th avenue by dirt roads with bushes on all sides of the roads for about two hundred feet before you got to the old houses on Sugar Hill. Our Cub Scout Den met on Sugar Hill every Tuesday afternoons for our little Cub Scout meetings. We often held outdoor cookouts in the woods there on Sugar Hill just off the dirt roads. One of the Cub Scouts, Big Eddy, was a resident of Sugar Hill, and he was the leader of the Sugar Hill gang.

The gang was comprised of little boys and girls and was more like the gang that couldn't shoot straight, and a club house joke. We tried to get the Big Eddy the gang leader to disband the gang, but he refused, and made arrangements for his gang to attack us after one of our Cub Scout meetings. We had to walk down the dirt roads with bushes on all sides in order to get back to 9th Avenue and go home. We didn't like walking down those dirt roads as it was getting dusk because there were no lights, just bushes.

As our Cub Scout meeting ended we noticed that our fellow scout and gang leader Big Eddy started running to go home we assumed. We took our time leaving the meeting and we were peacefully strolling down the dirt roads on our way to 9th Avenue to go home. As we got too far down the dirt road to turn around, all of a sudden Big Eddy and his gang members stood up from the bushes on both sides of the road and began to throw rocks, brick bats, and everything they could pick up at us.

We saw that we were outnumbered and trapped, so we began to run down the dirt road toward 9th avenue thinking that we would be safe if we could reach 9th avenue less than two hundred feet away. To our surprise Big Eddy and his gang kept following us and throwing everything at us that they had. They had even pre-positioned their rocks, brick bats, etc. all up and down the sides of the dirt road leading all the way to 9th Avenue. I wanted to stand and fight but the older Cub Scouts said that we should keep going and just get away from this area.

We successfully reached 9th Avenue which was a big paved street, and we went up 9th Avenue about a block to where it runs into Race Path Avenue, thinking that they would not follow us into our neighborhoods. To our surprise they kept following us, all of them, the boys and the girls, just picking up rocks and brick bats as they found them, and throwing them at us. I got tired of running and looked for Big Eddy the gang leader, and I saw him there bending over to get something to throw at us.

I looked around for something to get my hands on, and I saw a sun dried hard brick bat just lying there near the fork in the road of 9th Avenue and Race Path Avenue. I reached down and picked up the hard brick bat and I threw it in the direction of Big Eddy the gang leader as he was still bending down. The hard brick bat hit Big Eddy squarely in the temple, maybe just a little off center. I threw it really hard just like I was throwing a baseball from shortstop to first base. Even before he stood up Big Eddy the gang leader began to hold his head and cry profusely. All of the other gang members stopped and stood still and didn't throw anything else at us. They were clearly stunned to see their so called leader as a little cry baby, and they just stood there saying nothing and doing nothing.

Finally Big Eddy's older sister said that she saw me throw the brick bat that hit her brother in the head, and that she was going to the police station and tell the police. There was a neighborhood police station on highway 378 just a block up from Race Path Avenue. We decided to let her go, as the older Cub Scouts with us told me not to worry because it was

Big Eddy's Sugar Hill Gang that started the trouble by attacking us first and we were only acting in self defense.

We don't know what happened to Big Eddy's gang after that, and the police never came and the gang went out of existence. The gang never confronted us again as we walked down the dirt roads with bushes on all sides leaving Sugar Hill. I felt a great deal of accomplishment for having a reputation for being known as the little guy that got rid of the Sugar Hill Gang. And even to this day as I ride through the Sugar Hill neighborhood I still think of what happened there over a half century ago when the roads were all dirt roads in that little section of town.

Today some of my best friends and classmates from high school still live in the Sugar Hill section of town. So Big Papa I'm telling you this story so that you can see that sometimes self defense is warranted and justified. Big Papa just smiled and said, well your actions probably made it safer for me to live there because you had already gotten rid of a major problem, and maybe we all do have something in common. And there really is a lot that we can learn from each other right here under the old oak tree way back here in our little country community, so lets' continue to share our experiences and revelations with each other.

Big Papa's Revelations – Big Papa rose up on the bench a little and stated that he has heard many similar inspiring stories right here under the old oak tree over the decades. That he also sat under this same old oak tree as a little child growing up and listening to his mother and grandmother and granddad tell such stories right here under the old oak tree. The mothers' of the prior generation knew that they had few and limited schools in the area for their children, and encouraged their children to learn from some of the elders there under the old oak tree. Children could stay out past sunset under the old oak tree because the parents knew that some of the old timers didn't get off work until late, and would take a little rest there under the old oak tree listening to and telling stories well after sunset.

They sometimes needed a little rest before continuing on to their little country community way back there across the river. One could also get a special type of rejuvenation there under the old oak tree, that you just couldn't seem to get anywhere else. Some of the women would come there early on weekends and start preparing for a little cookout to celebrate various occasions throughout the year. There was always a birth or marriage, homecoming, etc. to celebrate, as big families were quite normal back then. These gatherings were a place and time for the youngsters to see and receive certain practices and traditions as they were being passed down from the prior generation. Practical skills were taught and passed down right there, as well as survival skills being taught, such as, how to survive off the land including farming, hunting and fishing, as well as plowing and planting, and taking care of the live stocks, so that one can become self sufficient and independent.

The youngsters were eager to learn, and knew that their little small isolated schools could not teach them everything they needed to know. They became accustomed early on to adjust to being taught in the churches and homes, especially homes of the teachers and at the Big House as every isolated community had a place they referred to as the Big House in the community, and was a place where the elders often met to exchange ideas, strategies, or socialize.

The women of the community often met at the Big House on certain days while the men were getting together under the Old Oak Tree. The women would discuss situations that required special skills and the nurturing of females. This was essential to maintaining a good family life on their way back isolated community. In such physical isolation, the families are all they have, and is your emergency 911 so to speak. The women made sure that everyone was being properly taken care of, and some of them had some excellent homegrown remedies, including herbal treatment, and knew how to cook certain things the proper way. There were many parenting skills, economic and artistic skills that were passed down to them from the prior generation, unto this very day.

At times you may see them planting certain vegetables in their garden, or see them making soap in the big pot in the back yard under a tree. They made their own ice cream, and would also make butter by churning it. They made baskets and wicker chairs and some furniture for their houses, and made refreshments from the berries and pies from the apple and pear trees, etc. It was all considered in a day's work, and then came the wonderful evenings in which it was time to pause and reflect.

Then they would all meet at sunset under the old oak tree to watch the setting sun disappear beyond the river's horizon, and listen to some more old stories as they relaxed. It's a time to have some refreshments, desert after dinner or a snack, or whatever one needs to help them relax after such a hard day's work way back here in this old isolated country community. This is the way life has been here down home for generations in spite of all the modern conveniences in the world today.

Big Papa tells the story of how it was right here under the same old oak tree that he was able to really solidify his relationship with his future wife. Although they all were from right there on that isolated island beyond the mighty river, they were from different small villages and Big Papa says he was a little shy a half century ago when she caught his special eye. He was about fifteen years old and she was a few years younger, and Big Papa could never get up enough courage to approach her directly as all the children walked to school from their little villages on the other end of the island. She was a cute little doll as Big Papa tells the story so many decades later. She was not really shy but it was customary for little girls not to approach little boys too strongly back in those days, especially if the little girl's father didn't know what was going on and didn't approve of you talking to his little girl without his express permission.

Big Papa said he could never muster up enough courage for his very special approach as they were walking those old sandy roads going to and from school. Big Papa knew that on Friday and Saturday nights there were always many of the children that came to sit under the big old oak tree to hear the elders tell stories of life and times gone by. The old oak tree was so special that it always seemed to have a special pull or spiritual reflection for Big Papa, and he felt completely at ease under the old oak tree at sunset and asked questions automatically as stories were being told.

On this particular early Friday evening Big Papa arrived a little early and got himself set up in a good spot with an extra seat near him. As the sun started to go down sure enough the little girls came and Big Papa to this day has not revealed how he got his little special cutie to take the seat beside him. But as the story goes Big Papa ended up not only getting to ask a lot of questions but also explaining some of the stories and events to the little cutie sitting right there beside him. There still is something special and miraculous about sitting there in that environment under the old oak tree after sunset. Big Papa still swears to that all these decades later, and he recalls how he got to explain stories and events to his little cutie all the way back across the river to their little villages way back on the back side of that old isolated island.

He made sure she got home safely and her parents began to like Big Papa, and trusted him to escort their little girl to and from meetings under the old oak tree. The rest is history now as Big Papa and his little cutie had a big little island church wedding back there over a half century ago. They are still living a wonderful life there among serene and pristine beauty tucked there way back in time. They are still recalling their fond memories of their life and times there under the old oak tree so many decades ago; it's still a miracle to them.

A Special Miracle – There under that very special old oak tree, especially at sunset, there seems to be a special spiritual pull and connection to the area there that keeps bringing people back. Even generations who have moved away to live and work keep coming back to reunions and various other events, and you'll see them at some point in time spending time there under the old oak tree. They sit there just like they did so many years ago growing up in our little isolated country community still tucked away way back in time. Many of them are even bringing their children with them to listen to the many stories that are still being told today right there at sunset under the old oak tree. Many of their children have spent their entire young lives in the big cities, having been born there. After a while even these little city children seem to really reconnect in a very special way.

It is quite apparent that their parents had taught them well about their life and times there at sunset under the old oak tree, as it too is a big and special part of their culture and history. Their parents are passing down certain customs and traditions to them just as it was passed down from their ancestors over the years.

As the sun sets over the river's banks you can hear in the distance the sound of a lone motor as one of the last boats is headed across the river to go home. And even if work kept them a little late they'll usually stop and spend at least a little time here under the old oak tree. They'll either have a story to tell, or may just want to listen and rest awhile. Here right before our eyes is a unique communication channel and grapevine that is really getting information and advice to the people in real time, and is right on time and essential to their survival and way of life.

It seems that no matter where people go or find themselves at the moment, they just have to come back to their reunions here at this very special place. And as they leave you can see their reflections in the last sunset, just there going down beyond the banks of the mighty river. Their unique culture and lifestyle has taught us all a very valuable lesson.

The old man has seen many sunsets sitting under the old oak trees. Just before the sun goes all the way down he goes to the water's edge by the riverbank to see his reflection in the last sunset.

A Reflection By The Water's Edge

The Old Man's Reflection
In The Last Sunset

The old man is the most senior elder in this way back down home community on an old isolated pristine island along the coast of the Carolina Lowcountry. He was born and raised on the old isolated island and has spent his entire life there except for his service in World War II. He lives right there in the Big House by the bank of the Waccamaw River, and he watches the sun sets each day as he sits under the big old oak tree, just as he has for decades. I asked him what's so unique about just watching the sun set over the river's horizon. The old man just kept staring at his reflection in the river as the sun was fading, paused a little and then he said.

As I sit here under this old oak tree as the sun sets late in the evening here on the bank of that mighty and ferocious black Water River, I can look closely and see reflections in the last sunset even as it fades away beyond the distant horizon. It's as if good memories are fading away right before your eyes. But such good memories will not be lost forever because the reflections will be embedded within your memory forever for it's a deep part of your culture and heritage. I have lived out this scene and experiences many times before along with other residents here in this way back in time little country community. Many generations before us have had these experiences right here under this same old oak tree, especially at sunset.

Stories have been passed down from generation to generation, and even those who have moved away decades ago still return on a yearly basis just to renew the spirit of their mind with this very unique spot here under the old oak tree. It's here that the elders still tell their stories and pass along a little wisdom of the ages based on their experiences of life. Fathers' still bring their sons to experience this unique form of learning that they will not get anywhere else, even though many of the youngsters now have the opportunity to go to good colleges and universities to get a good education and economic skills. It may seem strange to some to accept or believe that these old elders can still impart knowledge to some of these youngsters with multiple degrees from some institutions of higher learning.

As the old man explained it, "there is nothing new under the sun", as stated by Ecclesiastes or the Preacher millenniums ago. Therefore, what one generation gets by going to institutions of higher learning, the prior generation got from a different or higher source. Some of the youngsters may get a little frustrated after getting multiple degrees, yet remain unable to impart knowledge or understanding to some of the elders. One of the elders put it very plainly when he said I have seen many sunsets over the decades, and analyzed certain events that occurred during my days and I have seen it all. Many things are not what they appear to be and not necessarily what someone tells you it is; but when you experience it for yourself you will know exactly what it is and whether it is good for you.

The old man has a very deep faith, but cautioned that you must be able to distinguish "true faith" from foolishness, and fact from fiction, or you could be very easily mislead by vain persons. The art of discernment comes with true faith, knowledge and understanding, and that is a major reason the elders keep coming back to this spot under the old oak tree to keep imparting their experiences to the younger generation. Each time that I go back to visit I always go to the meetings and get together under the old oak tree just to renew the spirit of my mind.

Many of the very deep memoirs comes back and I can still see the old man's reflection in the last sunset, long after the sun has gone down and set over the bank of the mighty black water river. Deep over the horizon you can just feel him still imparting his knowledge and experiences deep into the night to us here in our little sacred spot under the old oak tree. Some of the parents being away in the city working for decades may not have had the time to bring their little children back here too often where their roots are deeply embedded. But there will be events or traumatic events that will invariably drive them back to their roots for more of that down home spiritual guidance. These are the types of intuitive guidance the elders have known about for generations.

Intuitive Guidance – One of the fathers that had moved away to the city had a young son with multiple degrees, and they had not come back home under the old oak tree for a few years. The young son had assumed he was an expert in investing and had fallen for an on-line investment scam by one of the post Katrina con artists selling bogus investments. The con artist fed the youngster the convoluted truth about making big money on foreclosed homes due to the hurricane along the coast. The con artist made and did some smooth talking and got the youngster to max out his credit card on-line. The youngster had no real idea of what he was getting into, and later thought he was making a loan to help purchase some foreclosed property to sell, and that he would get a portion of the profits. Con artists have been duping weary investors for years, and are now actively targeting the youngsters who believe they are highly educated and have expertise. The con artist was so good and effective that the youngster never got any evidence to show that the con artist engaged in any illegal activity whatsoever.

As it turned out the con artist had effectively duped a large number of investors out of a lot of money. The con artist had set up a number of limited liability companies (LLC) legally. The con artist controlled all of the companies and apparently placed the duped investor's money into the various companies, as this is all legal and looks legitimate in form.

As an old tax shelter worker I recognized the great potential for the promoter (con artist) to make related party transactions with the various companies that would not all be "arms length transactions". The potential for someone with an ulterior motive to steal the money and not get caught is clearly red flagged. There are about as many ways to steal the money in the companies controlled by the con artist as there are duped investors waiting to get cleaned out. The con artist can put the investor's money into certain companies and have the companies make loans to other companies owned by the con artist, loans that are never repaid. The con artist can have his company purchase foreclosed properties and sell the foreclosed properties at fair market value to the companies that have the duped investor's money in it. Many other schemes are possible and could and probably were done, as no one will ever know for sure except the con artist, and it's a known fact that they will never tell.

And now that the youngster knows that his money is gone for good, he's having a hard time believing that he got duped with his multiple degrees. As it turned out the con artist was using a vacant lot in a subdivision as an address with a telephone number is no longer in service. It appears that the con artist is still misleading some of the duped investors by telling them that the devastated hurricane also put them out of business. But a legitimate business would have a post Katrina business address and a working telephone number. The Better Business Bureau has no information on the alleged business. These companies were set up legally and it appears that the proper filings were made with the state, but this does not regulate or insure that immoral persons or prevent them from stealing your money.

The youngster now has something to learn from the old man that he should have learned years ago if his father had only brought him here under the old oak tree to listen and learn. The old man would have seen right through that scheme, for there is nothing new under the sun. The old man had heard stories of how his ancestors had lost many acres of land to similar schemes over the decades. Youngsters who are willing to listen and learn will not continue to make the same mistakes of the past because they will have a good knowledge of their history and culture. To move forward with ease one should know the pitfalls of the past, for they are also on the road to forward progress for the young generation.

When the old man heard everything that the youngster had done, he paused and reflected, and then he said I don't have multiple degrees, but I can separate and distinguish "fact from fiction" and "faith from foolishness". I have seen it all before and we should practice the "art of discernment". We all should know that there is no free ride, and that we must Study and Work (I Thessalonians 4:11, II Thessalonians 3:10-12). I know the Value of Work, in addition to faith. We should all go to school and learn as much as we can as man has some very good schools and institutions of higher learning. We can get many things from man and man can teach us much; but there are some things that we only receive by revelation (Galatians 1:12).

The old man of wisdom, as we call him, has been plowing and planting for generations, and he still receives a good harvest each year. He knows that it's a surety; that you can only reap what you sow (Galations 6:7). He has seen many a seasons come and go, and has journeyed into deep, deep waters over the years. He knows that the flesh man that lives under the sun has but a short time to tarry here, and must be prepared to meet the challenges along the way. The old man said that one's sojourn and life here is like a passing shadow and will not abide here long, and can be gone with the setting sun.

We must all Study and Work hard to insure that our sojourn here is not in vain. There is a great deal that we all can learn from the past if we will but stop and listen to those who have gone through so much and have survived intact with a renewed 'spirit of the mind", a new mindset, the "new man". That is why it is imperative that we continue to return to this part of our roots right here under the old oak tree, here by the water's edge near the banks of the mighty and ferocious black water river.

Words of wisdom, and stories of old are still passed down by the elders who have seen it all over the decades. The elders know that certain reflections of the past will give you guidance and knowledge that's still valid today. Most of the old timers know very well the story of the early days when they were going to grade school with the wonderful little Miss "Felee" a legend in her own time. The old man and the elders said there is a lesson to be learned here, and they often reflect on their young days so many decades ago.

Little Miss Felee – The old man said that Miss Felee was about the prettiest little girl in our way back country community over a half century ago. Our little section was located about a mile and a half from the school on the other end of the old isolated island. We all had to walk to school in those days as there were no motor vehicles on our little side of the old isolated island. The little boys and little girls always walked to school together in groups of about a half dozen or so for protection and to keep each other company. All the little boys took special notice of little Miss Felee early on as she was a special sight to behold, a beautiful and shining princess.

All the little boys wanted to talk to her and make her their own, and jockeyed for a position near her on our trips and walks to and from school. She appeared to be extremely shy or so we thought or were led to believe that she was so shy. Every time one of the little boys would get too close to her or talked to her for too long she would dash into the woods that lined the sandy roads along the way to school. She would remain in the woods and walk in the woods until we got near our destination, and then she would come out of the woods to rejoin us as we all continued on.

The little boys would always try to join her on her walk through the woods, but soon as the boys entered the woods after her she would always lose them. She could run faster than all the little boys and knew all the good hiding spots along and off the beaten trails in the woods. We assumed that she was just shy, but on many occasions there in the woods and along the way it sure enough seemed like she was just playing with us and teaching the little boys a lesson. The little boys naturally thought that they could catch her and find her in those woods, but each time she left them on the sandy roads and entered the woods they were lost before they started to try to find her. But we always followed after her because all the little boys wanted to make her their most fine and beautiful princess.

The woods were a little thick in spots and if you were not too familiar with them someone could blend in with the woods not too far from you and you wouldn't be able to see them until they moved a little. As we followed her into the woods I was absolutely certain that I could run just as fast as she could and keep up with her. But her fast dash was faster and quicker than all the little boys, and she would make a mad dash to one of her hiding spots and we'd spend all of our energy running around and still not knowing that she was probably there nearby resting and smiling as we expended our energy. We'd often see nothing but bushes moving as she got up and ran farther from us while we were too tired to run as fast as she was running, so we never caught her after she entered the woods.

It took us a while to accept the fact that this fine little princess could outfox, outrun, and outwit all us little boys. Sometimes she wouldn't rejoin us near our destination by coming out of the woods, she would just continue on to our destination, such as our school and be sitting there in class with that shy smile on her face as we entered our little country classroom.

It wasn't until many years later that it became very apparent to most of us that the apparently shy little Miss Felee was not shy at all, but may have just playing tricks on us and teaching us a lesson. After all these years she still comes to this little spot right here under the old oak tree listening to and telling stories that happened so many years ago. The little boys are now older men and to this day she has not told them how she lost them in the woods. So the old timers keep wondering today as they watch Miss Felee tells stories and gives insights to a new generation of little girls. The little girls are very attentive as Miss Felee teaches them, and from a distance it appears that they giggle at something Miss Felee tells them now and then.

The little girls don't tell anyone what Miss Felee told them that made them giggle, but insist that they have learned a lot and gotten insights on how to handle certain situations especially when it comes to little boys. Miss Feelee and the little girls still sit there listening to and telling stories late into the evening long after the sun has set over the river's horizon. Some say they stay so late just to see the reflections of the little boys in the last sunset, and the little boys are now older men after so many sunsets over the decades. But the reflections don't change much and the lessons to be learned never change much and are relevant to each new and succeeding generation, for they will encounter the same challenges of life in different forms, etc.

The old man of wisdom has told us this many times before, as told and taught to him by his Big Papa. And now even though most of the old timers have died out, those who are left still come to this little spot right here under the old oak tree. We can see and feel the old man's reflection in the last sunset as it fades anciently over the horizon far beyond the bank of the black water river. I can still hear his words of wisdom after all these years telling me and giving me valuable insights so many years ago that are still valid today.

Their fortitude is still here with us as we sojourn in the paths they so ably tread decades ago. Their lifestyle is reflected in us as we carry on in their magnificent tradition, and journey out into even deeper waters. We were taught how to analyze the situation and carefully analyze the facts and carefully define the problem and act accordingly. As I pause and reflect it becomes easier to see the lessons they imparted to us in their unique way, right there under that old oak tree.

Many people still come each and every year to this out of the place area we consider very special, and reflect on seeing the old man's reflections in the last sunset as they remembered it so many decades ago. I know that I will never forget the many experiences that I had here as a young child growing up in this special area. The legacy is continuously passed down to the youngsters and children, and some of them look forward to coming back each and every year with their parents to relive the experiences their parents told them about.

If you look closely out over the river's horizon you can still see the old man's reflection in the last sunset. He was among a truly unique generation in these tucked away communities on the Carolina Lowcountry.

The old man sees his reflection in the river at the last sunset, and knows that subsequent generations must also take a Journey into Deep, Deep Waters, and will need guidance from a higher source in Overcoming the many obstacles along life's journey.

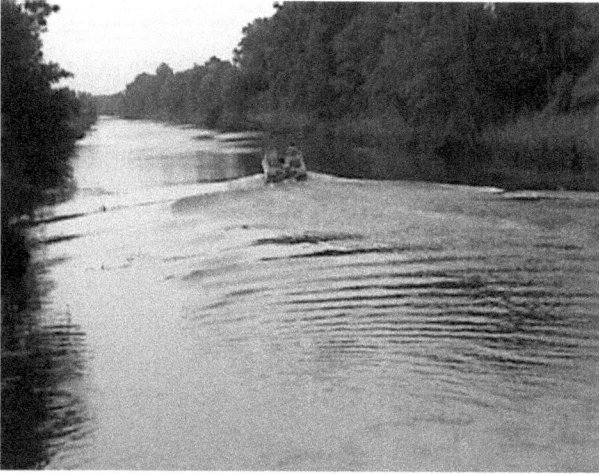

A Journey Into Deep, Deep Waters

A Journey Into Deep, Deep Waters

There are many rivers along the coast of the Carolina Lowcountry, and some of the rivers flow into the Atlantic Ocean. Rivers surround that old isolated pristine island that is known as Sandy Island. Many residents live near the banks of the Waccamaw River on the island, and the most senior elder sits on his front porch or under the old oak tree and watch the river as it goes roaring downstream on its way to the ocean. Residents often wade into the shallow parts of the river near the bank of the river, but they're not to wade in too deeply because the currents can very easily carry you out into the deeper waters which flows downstream into the ocean. The most senior elder is known as "the old man" and he constantly tell those nearby, especially the youngsters that life itself is like a journey into deep, deep waters. The old man sat and told the youngsters that he never went out into the deep part of the river without being adequately prepared; and that in life you can't go too far without being prepared to be successful.

The old man moved his chair closer to the banks of the river, looked at the youngsters and said, I am approaching the century mark and I   sit quietly each day under the old oak tree, and enjoy the peace and tranquility of this special area here on this old pristine isolated island. I sit quietly and peacefully by the bank of the mighty black water river, and reflect on years and times gone by decades ago. As I stroll down from the big house each day I look forward to telling more stories and pass on a little wisdom of the ages. I have seen many generations come and go as well as some fundamental changes in the society at large. I'm usually the first to arrive here under this old oak tree and stay well past sunset, and have seen many reflections in the last sunset as it recedes over the horizon beyond the water's edge at the banks of the river.

One of the youngsters asked the old man; just what is the secret to your longevity as you still walk briskly all over this little portion of the isolated island. The old man calmly replied, well you live and you learn, but step one is always the same no matter what your goals or objective; be prepared and then take action to accomplish the task. Life you see is like a journey into deep, deep waters, and before you journey out into the deep waters you should be prepared. I spent many years learning in the shallow waters of the inlet because in such shallow waters you can see clearly to the bottom of the waters. You can see what to step on and what to avoid, and even see what's swimming around in the shallow waters. You can perfect your swimming strokes and life saving techniques before you venture into the deeper waters.

I perfected my techniques in the shallow waters of the inlets before I ventured into crossing the mighty and ferocious black water river in the little row boats, where everything in the river is very murky. Just as you must be prepared for the unknowns of the deep waters when crossing the river, you must be prepared for the unknown challenges of life as you venture out into the world. We can learn a lot from our ancestors and elders, but at some point in life we must all venture out and confront and overcome the challenges and obstacles that are inherently a part of life as we sojourn along in this weary land.

That is the main reason that I continue to return to this spot under the old oak tree to pass on the stories of life that I have experienced for almost a century. The elders before me passed on such stories and insights of life to me as I was growing up here, and such wisdom and truth guided me well over the decades and have brought me to this very day. I know that the young people of today are different in many ways, as they must live and compete in a highly technological 21st century society amid many cultures in the global economy. They also face the pull and persuasion of their peers, which is not always in their best interest.

Therefore, they must be thoroughly prepared to compete in such a vastly different world than their elders. It is extremely imperative that they understand the economic struggles of their elders in their pursuit to succeed, as the basic fundamental lessons are still relevant today. It is even truer today that if the young generation forgets their history, they will surely repeat it today in this global economy. The elders have seen it all and can save the youngsters some headaches and pitfalls, as step one is always the same, "be prepared"! There is always a main theme of the old man as he sits and passes down his experiences to the younger generation under the old oak tree. He gives them some fundamental lessons in stories form so that they can more easily remember the fundamental lesson within the story.

The old man leaned back in his chair and began to tell the youngsters the story of how he had to live off the land during his young days, as there were little or no economic opportunities available to them here on the isolated island along the Lowcountry. There were some lean years and some bad storms and hurricanes over the years. Some of which washed away some parts of the inlets and property lines. These events on the isolated island helped him to be prepared when he was drafted to serve in World War II so very far from home. The old man remembers riding on the big ship across the Pacific Ocean, and says that one of his best sights was returning and seeing their ship come in under the Golden Gate Bridge. His struggles and fortitude on this isolated island had prepared him well for his duties overseas and elsewhere.

The old man says he is still certain that the experiences on the old pristine island will teach and give even the younger generation the preparation that they will need to succeed, as they venture out into the larger world to compete. The old man tells the story of one of his young descendants, Robbie, who moved away from the island in search of a better life and more opportunities. Robbie moved away to a big city to work his way through college. He took a big Greyhound Bus out of town as it was all he could afford at that time, and after riding the bus for many hours he arrived in the big city. Robbie stayed with a relative who had left the island two decades earlier. Robbie was impressed with the big city and its faster paced lifestyle, and it took him a little while to adjust to the city neighborhood.

A Different Neighborhood – Robbie got a job in the big city and began to blend into his new environment, but always felt a little odd and didn't enjoy some of the things the other city youngsters were doing in the neighborhoods. The city youngsters tended to run or hang out in groups and did things their own way, as they had no use for their elders' advice and didn't accept advice. Robbie would always question their actions and was always told that he didn't have any rank, and to just keep quiet and do as he was told. The city groups were always headed by boys who had dropped out of school, and the girls in the group had certain specific limited roles at different times and events. Some of the things that they were into were not very pleasant or desirable, and offended many people.

Robbie the island youngster would always remember the advice of the old man under the old oak tree, and remembered that the old man said don't venture out into the deep, deep waters until you are adequately prepared to protect and help yourself. The old man always reminded us that there was always a lineup of vain persons out there just waiting to mislead unprepared people. Robbie did not want to start going down the long road to nowhere fast, and began to reflect on the wisdom he received by the water's edge under the old oak tree just a few years earlier. Robbie came to the big city with a renewed spirit of the mind, and he could clearly see that the group of city youngsters hanging out in the city neighborhoods was heading into deep, deep waters unprepared.

Robbie began to look for other events and outlets in or near his neighborhood that would offer him an opportunity to get into something a little more productive. A recreation complex that was nearby had some softball fields, and Robbie loved to play baseball, and joined a team at the complex. Robbie was a natural middle infielder and could really turn that double play. The softball team was actually a coed softball team, and a slender young female outfielder caught Robbie's special eye. It was just a matter of time, just a few innings so to speak, until Robbie and Ruthie the attractive outfielder became best friends and a winning combination. They were both a little shy and supported each other in every aspect and were admired by all their teammates and friends. They confided in each other and Ruthie was always there offering her support and advice to Robbie.

Ruthie lived in a neighborhood across town and was also familiar with the neighborhood that Robbie was living in, as she was a lifelong resident of the city and had attended its public schools and colleges. One nice quiet evening they were strolling quietly in the park that was right beside the softball complex. Robbie asked Ruthie if he could ask her advice about some of the things that were going on in his neighborhood, as he was getting even more concerned about some of the things the youngsters were contemplating. Ruthie quickly recognized that trouble was looming in Robbie's neighborhood and quietly arranged for them to spend more time in her neighborhood, as she knew of many nice places in her neighborhood that Robbie would enjoy with her.

Ruthie recognized that Robbie was being set up to tread out into deeper waters, and could very easily end up down the long road going nowhere fast. They both were avid sports fans and enjoyed researching on the internet. Ruthie conveniently arranged for Robbie to help her in some on-line research for a little sports booklet she was putting together. Robbie began to spend more time with Ruthie at her house doing research on-line. With the two of them working on the booklet, the project began to go very well. They became even closer together and were beginning to become just more than good friends. Robbie began to spend less time in his old neighborhood hanging out with the youths in his area.

This didn't play well with the young leaders of the neighborhood group and they were determined to teach the young country boy Robbie a city lesson. The leaders assigned a couple of bigger thugs to follow Robbie and find out where and who he was spending his time with. The bigger thugs followed Robbie to Ruthie's part of town and realized that it was another rival group's turf, so to speak. They decided to teach Robbie a lesson after following him to Ruthie's house. But unbeknownst to the bigger thugs Ruthie had been looking out her window and noticed that Robbie was being followed and probably being set up.

A Set Up – As Robbie was about to leave Ruthie's house after dinner, Ruthie noticed that the bigger thugs car was still sitting there just down the street. Ruthie suspected a set up against Robbie and decided to put herself right smack into the middle of the rumble. She walked out with Robbie and had in her hidden pockets some mace and a small 22 caliber pistol that she had a permit for. As Robbie and Ruthie walked down the dimly lit street they didn't see anyone, but Ruthie could feel that the bigger thugs were nearby and was prepared for any eventuality. As they got into Robbie's car and drove about a half block the rear tire became flat. As they got out to see what was wrong the bigger thugs jumped Robbie and placed him in the back seat of their car. Ruthie began screaming and acting hysterical and kept running to the car and the bigger thugs also put her in the back seat beside Robbie. They took her purse but didn't notice her hidden pockets as she had concealed those pockets well.

They drove to an industrial area in a very secluded part of town, and stopped the car on a very dark street. They forced Robbie and Ruthie out of the car and pushed them to the side of the dark street. Robbie was forced out of the car first so Ruthie had time to reach into her hidden pockets and get some mace. As they were taking Robbie to the other side of the dark street, Ruthie sprayed the inside of the car well with the mace. The bigger thugs left Robbie and Ruthie on the side of the dark street in the industrial area. As they were leaving to get back into their car Ruthie also sprayed over their heads in the dark night.

The bigger thugs jumped into their car and sped away very fast, thinking that they had done a number on Robbie and Ruthie. They drove less than half a block before there was a very loud screeching and screams calling for help. Ruthie told Robbie what she had done and gave Robbie the gun, and she kept the mace as they approached the bigger thugs on the ground screaming. They took the bigger thugs cell phones and called the police, as they knew that the car was probably stolen. The police and the ambulance arrived within a few minutes, and the thugs were treated and taken to jail. Robbie and Ruthie watched the events from a safe distance away in the dark, and the dumb thugs never told the police that anyone else was around, they may have been disoriented by the mace.

The bigger thugs never returned to Ruthie's neighborhood again, although one of them may still be in jail as he had numerous warrants. Robbie began to appreciate Ruthie even more and began to show her more and more attention, as he was still learning the ins and outs of the big city lifestyle. Robbie began to trust Ruthie even more, and began to tell her more about his life growing up in a way back country community, way beyond the ferocious black water river along the Carolina Lowcountry. He told her about the meetings and get-togethers they had under the old oak tree they had back home, and how stories were passed down from the elders. And that how in her he had seen a reflection of the lifestyle he had left behind on his old isolated island. Ruthie became more and more intrigued and was so curious that Robbie promised to take her on a trip back down home in the coming months. Ruthie knew that she had some roots deep down in the south as one of her grandparents was born in the south, and Ruthie's mom spent a few years growing up in the south before coming to the city with her mother as a young child.

A Trip South – Ruthie had remembered some of the things that her mother had told her about growing up in the south in a small rural area, but Ruthie was too young to remember much about her experiences visiting there so young. Ruthie knew from her mother's upbringing that there was something different and very special about those people down along the coast of the Carolina Lowcountry. Perhaps that is how she recognized the special qualities in Robbie, and went the extra efforts to help him in his hour of distress.

Robbie appreciated what Ruthie had done to save him and he began to prepare and save a little extra because he wanted to strike up the nerve to ask Ruthie to take a visit to the old isolated island. After a few months had passed and it was beginning to get springtime Robbie began to smell the roses each time he saw Ruthie. He knew that there was a modern vacation resort along the Atlantic ocean about four miles from the old isolated island where Ruthie could enjoy the beaches along with all the other tourists. In fact it was where a lot of the people on the island went to play tourist every now and then. Robbie often spent some of his vacation at the resort when he was not on the island. Robbie had the resort by the ocean send him a brochure of what they had to offer vacationers. The brochure that Robbie received was very smooth as the resort was marketing itself as a good place for a family vacation and offered various packages for everyone's budget.

One quiet evening as the sun was going down Robbie showed the brochure to Ruthie and told her it was not too far from the old isolated island. That it was indeed a 21st century resort with tennis courts, golf courses, fitness centers, etc. and was right there in the area with so much other history nearby that she would also enjoy. Ruthie accepted Robbie's invitation and insisted on helping to pay for part of the trip, as she had known about the history of the Carolina Lowcountry to some degree. Her mother had given her some information and history of the area over the years, and she knew about the old plantations and old restored slave cabins, and some of the first school for freed slaves in the area at the Penn Center.

A few months later in early Summer Robbie and Ruthie were on the airplane approaching the Myrtle Beach International Airport, and coming in low above the Atlantic Ocean for a landing. Airplanes often go beyond the airport to circle and turn over the ocean and approach the runway from the ocean. I have taken that plane ride many a times and I especially enjoy that landing approach that takes us out over the ocean before we land.

Robbie and Ruthie were met at the airport by his relatives, and Robbie's aunt had a large house down the street from Robbie's parent's house. Robbie's aunt had prepared a room for Ruthie in her house, and insisted that Ruthie stay with her during her vacation here in the Carolina Lowcountry. Robbie's aunt was a very deeply religious lady and Ruthie felt right at home at her house. They spent a lot of time together at the local churches, and visiting some of the old historical sites, cemeteries and plantations. Ruthie very quickly began to enjoy the hospitality and laid back lifestyle of the area. The more she and Robbie toured the surrounding areas the more she began to think about relocating there.

Ruthie enjoyed the outings on the old pristine isolated island and the get-togethers under the old oak tree, where the elders still pass down stories at sunset. Ruthie was a cancer survivor and noticed that the local schools and colleges had excellent health care classes and offered degree programs. Ruthie's experience with cancer made her aware and dedicated to getting into the health care field to help others, as she liked helping people.

Ruthie became so intrigued with the area and its people that she became convinced that she would return and relocate to the area to live and work. Robbie sensed that Ruthie was becoming more and more attached to the area and its history, and mentioned that it would be a good place for them to start out again together. Ruthie paused for a moment, and then realized that Robbie was proposing to her, and she just said yes, yes. Robbie then reached into his pocket and pulled out the biggest engagement ring ever seen on the old isolated island, and a new day began and the rest is history.

Robbie and Ruthie are now bringing their little baby child under the old oak tree, especially at sunset to listen to the elders tell even more stories. Another generation is being taught and given wisdom and insights before they journey into the deep, deep waters, for they must be prepared well before embarking on such a journey. This is a deeply embedded part of their culture and history, and has always been passed down from generation to generation here on this way back out of the way little community on this old isolated island. Robbie now knows from firsthand experience that you should not take a journey into deep, deep waters until you are adequately prepared to survive its unknowns, and obstacles that may be hidden in the murky waters. That is a lesson well known by the people on that old isolated pristine island along the coast of the Carolina Lowcountry.

Their unique culture and lifestyle has taught us a very valuable lesson as we journey on Overcoming the obstacles along life's journey. As we overcome the many obstacles on our journey through these difficult days, we can pause and reflect on how far we've come and brighten the vision of where we're going. We are uniquely prepared for that long day of atonement, and journey by the water's edge and beyond.

Journey By The Water's Edge
A Spiritual Experience

Journey By The Water's Edge

As we take this journey here by the water's edge we should stop and listen to that choir that's deep within our conscience before we tread too deeply. For we must all take that journey by the water's edge one way or another.

A youngster was preparing to leave his little tucked away community here along the Carolina Lowcountry. He decided to take one last walk down by the riverside just to stand at the water's edge, to just pause and reflect. Life is like the water's edge, and the river can be very cruel, cold and unforgiving. He saw the river rising and knew why the river was rising. The river's currents can be very deceptive and misleading, one moment calm and peaceful, and the next very violent and treacherous. He knew that one must watch their step as they tread by the water's edge.

As he relocated across the country he knew that life can also be very treacherous and uncertain, trials and tribulations may come, and obstacles placed in your way. His past experiences in the Carolina Lowcountry had prepared him well for life here on the west coast. He knew that he would have to continue Overcoming the many obstacles on his wayfaring journey. He spent over three decades on the west coast and successfully retiring to pursue other interests.

A Spiritual Experience – A week or so before Thanksgiving in 1995 I experienced a throbbing pain in my back. The pain was intense and would move to various parts of my back. I went to the doctor for a complete examination, and the doctor checked me out, but could find nothing wrong. I knew something was moving in my back telling me something. This pain I could not bear. What needless pain we bear, all because we do not carry everything to God in prayer. It is better to trust in the Lord than to put confidence in man. We have been foretold all things!

I engaged in deep meditation and prayer, and asked for this burden to be lifted. In a few days the pain subsided and was gone! A few days later I had a spiritual dream. I saw this long ugly limousine coming through my neighborhood picking up people to take them to the airport. The driver of the limousine was the funeral director who had passed away some time ago.

The limousine stopped at my door to pick me up, but I had forgotten to pack my suitcase, so I couldn't go with them. I told them to go ahead and I'll take a taxi to the airport. I noticed some luggage was falling off the old ugly limousine, so I went out to attempt to put the luggage back on the limousine. But it started to rain, so I ran back to my front porch. Then I awoke and realized what a spiritual experience and awakening I had. The question that I needed an answer to was answered. It was such a spiritual awakening that on the Sunday after Thanksgiving I went to Brookings AME Church on 73rd Avenue in Oakland to give thanks and praise.

We must be sure who we're riding with and that we are proceeding in a pragmatic direction. Check out the driver and don't just jump on board expecting a free ride. The type of driver will tell you where they're heading. A funeral director's job is to drive people to the graveyard, not the airport. The devil will come for you in many disguises, so be careful so that you don't fall for his snares. Limousines go to the graveyard as well as to the airport, so make sure the one you're on is heading in the right direction.

As for me I will remain in Affinity with the Almighty! I will continue on my journey knowing that I can rely on a higher source for guidance in Overcoming the obstacles along life's way. We must all give an offering for the atonement of our souls. I know that we can make it safely through that Long Day of Atonement.

A Long Day of Atonement - As we approach the critical crossroads on our journey through uncertain times in these latter days, it is imperative that we see clearly and choose the right road when we arrive at the critical crossroads. We must be prepared to avoid or overcome the many obstacles along this journey. As we approach the end of the long day and the sun is setting low, some may fall by the wayside. Fight the good fight of faith, and the victory will be yours, and you shall reap the benefits of your struggle.

A Battleship in the City – I was in a slight sleep or daze. The vision I saw was near home. It was a huge battleship in the city. It was loaded with missiles pointed toward the sky. A clear and distinct voice spoke from the ship giving specific instructions about life and what pragmatic direction one should proceed in.

In a flash after giving instructions, the battleship turned around in the middle of the street and went its way. Even though the battleship was out of the water, it didn't appear to be out of its environment, as it had huge rear wheels that turned on a dime. It warned of things to come.

This is a latter day event, but we need not be afraid or worry if we are prepared. In the midst of the chaos and confusion that will come, we must remain focused on the straight and narrow, and proceed in a pragmatic direction. Things may seem calm and peaceful, but certain trials and tribulations will surely come. Therefore be prepared, be not afraid, because we have been foretold all things.

As I pause and reflect on years gone by and the days of old back yonder there along the Carolina Lowcountry. The experiences there by the water's edge have carried me through some difficult days and years. It's now getting late in the evening and I know that changes are coming.

Old Oak Trees in the Carolina Lowcountry

Come Now! It's Late in the Evening

It's Late in the Evening

Many years have gone by since those days of old so long ago there by the water's edge on the bank of the river. Much has changed over the years as times have changed and life is much different now for many people. There has been some long and burdensome days for many people all over the land, with additional stresses brought on by the events of the day. There is much more economic stress now because of economic uncertainties beyond the control of so many people struggling to survive. The vision of prosperity has become cloudy and many people are becoming more disappointed and disillusioned.

We may be in the midst of a very painful and prolonged economic stagnation, and without a clear vision it will be easy for some to go marching off the deep end of the cliff. Many keep missing the message or keep going down that long road going nowhere fast. We need only apply scriptural solutions, as the solution is in the scriptures. There is no new thing under the sun.

Sister Soldier was a neighbor of mine in the city, and I saw some of the many trials and tribulations she went through, and endured and made it back home again. It is possible to come back home again, no matter how long you've been out in the storm of life. Out there you will labor and become heavy laden, and never find the rest you are seeking and need. Sister soldier was brought up in a good neighborhood in a good family. She strayed from her roots and ran with the wrong crowd all over the wrong side of the city.

I often stood on my front porch in the city as it was getting late in the evening, and watched the sun set over the foothills. I would see Sister Soldier as she roamed the streets with others from my front porch just down from the shopping mall up from my house.

I knew that many of them had come from good homes in the area, as their parents still lived in the neighborhoods. Their parents had worked hard all their lives and struggled to stay above water, and now some of their children have strayed away into the wrong lifestyle. Some people may have thought that this was just another passing fad, but as God was being taken out of the schools things have continued to go downhill for many communities.

I saw the changes over the decades, and as I stood on my front porch all those decades observing the neighborhoods. I knew that if we did not change directions fast that many people would end up marching on off the deep end of the cliff. A change will come and now it's up to each individual to pause and reflect and decide how they will make a positive contribution to making things better where they are. We must all take that next step in a new direction renewed in the spirit of the mind. We can continue to overcome all obstacles, including economic obstacles.

A Painful and Prolonged Economic Stagnation -

We were told millenniums ago that difficult economic times would come to this latter generation. Amid all the chaos and confusion of the moment one wonders if the underpinnings of the financial system have been destroyed by fraud, greed and corruption in the corporate culture. There has been a tremendous breach of trust in the market, with overvalued loans, and overextended credit. This has led to an inflated standard of living with more foreclosures coming, as there is too much water on too many balance sheets and off balance sheets. Mortgage backed securities, asset backed securities, and various derivatives have been grossly overvalued; collateralized debt obligations (CDO's) have been over-rated by the rating agencies for the big Wall Street financial institutions.

A borrow and spend economy-credit card economy, with a low savings rate will eventually fall to its correct level that's not inflated. For every debit there must be a credit, otherwise the economy keeps spinning out of control in a death spiral; marching off the deep end into a very painful and prolonged Economic Stagnation..

We must be prepared to compete in the Global Economy, as there are other rising economies in the Global Economy. We must acquire the Economic Skills, training and rehabilitation needed to compete successfully in the Global Economy. We are in a spiritual war (Ephesians 6:11-13) and there is only One who can heal the land (II Chronicles 7:14). Deuteronomy 8:19-20, 28:13.

There must be a new mindset – put on the new man. Difficult times are coming (Ezekiel 7:19, Zephaniah 1:14-18, James 5:1-7).

A Luciferian Influence has permeated a large segment of the culture to this day. We are in a spiritual war, and this is the "fig tree" generation and we have been foretold all things (St. Mark 13:23, St. Matthew 24:25). One must ask themselves why so many people in the industry took so many steps to disaster down the long road going nowhere fast. Was there a Luciferian Influence in the process, or was it just blind greed and corruption, fraud and breach of trust. A careful analysis of the steps will give you the answer.

Loan officers, mortgage brokers, financial schemers, etc. creating and devising various dubious loan products designed to generate high fees for themselves. Loans to be made to people who are high risk borrowers with low credit scores, and to people who don't document their income, and submit false applications with respect to their incomes just to get a loan they don't qualify for and cannot repay. Appraisers will overvalue the property to be sold.

Subprime Loans – Made to many high risk borrowers, many of whom submitted false applications. Includes No Doc loans (no documentation of income). Includes many adjustable rate mortgages (ARM) many with low teaser rates that will reset to much higher rates within a stated time period. Option ARMs – Adjustable rate mortgages which also give the borrower the option to decide how much interest they will pay each month. Interest not paid each month is added to principal. Thereby increasing the amount of the loan principal owed.

Loan officers, mortgage brokers, financial schemers, etc. in concert with borrowers to sell them a home that is highly overvalued. Value of home overstated from the very beginning, therefore the Loan to Value Ratio (LTV) is well over 100% from the very beginning as there is too much water in the LTV ratio. The property was overvalued from the beginning just to peddle to the many borrowers who are hooked on this borrow and spend credit economy, and will easily overextend themselves as they have been using credit to live an inflated lifestyle well beyond their means.

Although for many these continue to be some very difficult times, we must continue to overcome all obstacles that may and will surface. We need just listen to that choir that's deep within our conscience and make the just decision. We need not all just keep marching toward the deep end of the cliff. We must put on the new man, renewed in the spirit of the mind.

A Renewed Spirit of the Mind -

As long as a man continues to look at things the same old way, he will continue to see what he sees through the same old mindset. This will only keep him where he is with the old mind no matter how young or old he is.

One must look through the thick dark clouds and see the vision of the "new man" with a new mindset. There is a process for the "liberation of the mind" with a new thought process. But as long as you continue in the ways of the world there will be no "renewed spirit of the mind". There is "only one way" (St. John 14:6). We must put on the new man with a new mindset and a new vision (Ephesians 4:23-24).

We need not remain in poverty (Proverbs 28:19, 12:11). The destruction of the poor is their poverty (Proverbs 10:15). We must Study and Work (I Thessalonians 4:11, II Thessalonians 3:6-12).

No one will give us a home, we must work for what we get, as we will all reap what we have sown (Galatians 6:7). We must plow and plant to have a good harvest (Proverbs 20:4). We are all rewarded according to our works (Psalm 62:12, Revelation 20:12, 22:12). The new man must be renewed in knowledge (Colossians 3:10).

A clear vision will facilitate a greater Overcoming in these uncertain and difficult times, and I often pause and reflect on my days by the water's edge so many decades ago. The knowledge I received from my parents gave me insight and the secrets to success here so far away from the Carolina Lowcountry.

Many Secrets for Success Were Passed
Along So Many Years Ago Here Along
The Carolina Lowcountry

SECRETS FOR SUCCESS

Acquire Economic Skills! Pray & Work
Go to School! – Stay in School!
Do For Self! – Forget About Shortcuts.
Acquire Expertise and Experience. Work Experience!

PRODUCTION:
Acquire Economic Skills!
Produce Quality Products & Services
Obtain Ownership & Control of
Economic Entities (Yours)

DISTRIBUTION:
Marketing – Advertising

CONSUMERS:
Retail
Turn Over $ Dollars in Your Community

- Remain Focused on Goals and Objectives.
- Use a Systematic and Step-by-Step Approach to complete huge tasks.
- Constantly Probe and Analyze – Utilize a Real Time Action Plan.
- Clearly Define the Problem and Carefully Analyze the Facts.

Don't be systematically manipulated into economic dependency on others outside the community. Acquire Economic Autonomy!

The Road to Success May Not Be Easy
at Times, But Continue Your Journey
and Reap a Good Harvest

We were told many years ago there by the Water's Edge to remain focused, and to Have Goals and a Vision. That we must continue to Overcome all obstacles and obtain our goals.

HAVE GOALS AND A VISION
Remain Focused on Goals and Objectives

A man must come out of darkness and find his way into the light; but if he relies on himself to find his way out he may linger forever in his darkness. We need not fear for we too have the covenant (Genesis 9:11 and Deuteronomy 9:11). And Christ is our High Priest (Hebrews 9:11).

We must remain focused on our Goals and Objectives, and keep your Goal in your Vision! From Concept to Completion!

Visualize from layout to development to successful completion, and keep working toward your Goals and Objectives!

Setbacks may come, and obstacles may be placed in your way, but, keep working toward your Goals and Objectives!

It may take a while to set and lay a complete and solid foundation, but don't despair, keep working toward your Goals and Objectives!

Maintain – Credibility and a Commitment to proceed and achieve, and you will succeed and achieve and produce a Quality Product.

You must have Credibility and a Commitment to proceed until you accomplish your Goals and Objectives.

If you maintain Credibility and Commitment, all else will come naturally.

Practice Financial Accountability

Financial Accountability is imperative for one's financial well-being, and should be based on a Pragmatic Economic Agenda. One must acquire the necessary economic skills (not just degrees) to obtain economic autonomy.

Economic Autonomy – To include the ownership and control of economic entities within your community. Have Long Term Goals that will enable you to become independent and self sufficient.

Economic Agenda – Determine what must be done and do what must be done for you to obtain economic independence! Establish Priorities and Act. Identify major problems that need to be resolved.

Financial Accountability – Be prudent and establish checks and balances, internal controls, to ensure your continued financial good health. Make sure that your Revenues are always greater than your Expenses. Monitor your Debits and Credits, and use T-Accounts if necessary. We must operate prudently in this 21st century electronic banking system that gives us easy access to ATM's and all types of credit and credit cards, as it is so easy to become overloaded with debt nowadays. Debt is the destruction of many.

Analyze financial statements, income statement and balance sheet, and make sure that the balance sheet is not overloaded. Make sure that your current assets to current liabilities ratio is sufficient. Avoid non-productive people and freeloaders.

Remember, you will retain no benefits without accepting and living up to your responsibilities and obligations!

Month _____

Income   **Expenses**

Make sure that your income is greater than your expenses, and your expenses should include your necessaries. To continue to spend more than you make leads to debt and major problems.

Month _____

Income	Expenses
	Mortgage-Rent
	Insurance
	Taxes
	Electricity
	Heat
	Water
	Garbage
	Telephone
	Clothes
	Cable TV
	Miscellaneous
	Emergency

Make sure that you have identified all you monthly bills, and also budget for other bills that are not due monthly but will have to be paid within the year, such as taxes and insurance. And you may have enough left for a vacation if you keep your credit card debt down and under control.

Practicing Financial Accountability was one of the subjects we were taught so many decades ago; to study and work and become self-sufficient and independent. Practice Financial Accountability and do not become one of the economically disenfranchised. These secrets for success were also instilled in us at the old Whittemore High School along the Carolina Lowcountry. They taught us the necessity to have goals and objectives, and to remain focused on achieving such goals and objectives. To have a plan with strategies and the means to accomplish such goals were critical. Otherwise it's just a dream that can't come true.

Many lessons were taught there in those little quaint out of the way isolated pocket communities, especially at the old Whittemore High School where there were some really dedicated teachers. The old school is demolished now, and a new middle school, Whittemore Park, now stands where the old Whittemore High School once stood.

Each time I went back to visit over the decades I would take time to stroll down by the water's edge, and sit under the old moss laden oak trees. I would also go to where the old Whittemore High School once stood to meditate and reflect on the days of old. A return to the Carolina Lowcountry was something I always looked forward to.

The Old Whittemore High School
Along The Carolina Lowcountry

A Return to the Carolina Lowcountry

After many decades away living on the west coast working, the youngster returned to the Carolina Lowcountry after retiring. I was that youngster who now returns to spend a few years by the water's edge, as the pull of the river brought me back to my roots. The passage of time has brought many changes to the area, especially much more development. But many of the old tucked away isolated communities still exist, some as they were decades ago.

That youngster that left the area so many decades ago is still in me; and I was eager to see and document the current customs, habits and folkways of the people there now. I wanted to see how things and traditions may have changed over the decades, especially with the younger generation. I wanted to see the old neighborhoods and communities, and see some of the people I went to school with who still reside in the area. Many of the tucked away isolated communities are where the Gullah people have resided for centuries.

The Gullah-Geechee culture is unique to the coastal areas and sea islands of the Carolinas, Georgia and Florida. It is known as Gullah in the Carolinas and as Geechee in Florida and Georgia. The Gullah-Geechee people are direct descendants of residents of West Africa's rice coast who were brought here as slaves to work the fertile coastal areas. When the captains of slave ships brought Africans to America, they dropped many of their captives off at Charleston, S.C. which was America's largest slave marketing center in the 18th century. It has been estimated that over one third of Blacks can trace their history to the Charleston seaport.

Many of the slaves were taken to plantations on the isolated barrier islands off the South Carolina coast. Many of the plantations were rice plantations along the waccamaw neck along the Waccamaw River. And even though stripped of their homeland and forced to live in isolated patches they continued to speak their language and retain their culture. The Gullah culture, handed down by West African slaves, is still alive on Sandy Island and the island communities along the South Carolina coast. For over 300 years the Gullah people have resided in these low lying isolated pockets. The lack of bridges to the islands left the Gullah culture unspoiled and pristine with its dominant motherland influences. The isolation retained their distinct cultural differences from mainland residents.

The Carolina Lowcountry has been home to the Gullah People for centuries. The Lowcountry consists of the coastal areas and Sea Islands, and the Lowcountry is known for its good fertile grounds. Some of the communities have changed, some are changing and some are gone. I was born and raised in South Carolina along the coast about 14 miles from the Atlantic Ocean, in the Old Historic Riverfront Town of Conway. My father was born and raised on Sandy Island, S.C., an isolated island that is still the home to some Gullah people.

The old communities and isolated areas are still there with a few of the old timers left; but a younger generation is on the timeline now. Life by the river today is different in many respects, with new obstacles to Overcome.

Life by the River Today

The Customs, Habits and Folkways of a People

The mighty Waccamaw River still flows along the Carolina Lowcountry and is a major black water river that has provided pleasure and food for generations. I journeyed away but kept feeling the pull of the river calling me home. The Gullah-Geechee people have a very rich history and culture that has remained virtually intact for centuries in their new land. The indigenous West African Cultural traditions survived, and are still flourishing today.

The customs, habits and folkways of the people of West Africa is alive today in the Carolina Lowcountry and Sea Islands. The good traditions have been passed down from generation to generation throughout the centuries. Tourists are flocking to the Carolina Lowcountry to visit the many plantations, etc. that offer guided tours of their historic sites. There is a wealth of history here all up and down the Carolina Lowcountry and various Sea Islands. There are various museums and events at the Penn Center on St. Helena Island during the year. In Charleston there are other archives, Old Slave Mart, etc. The old Atlantic Beach is still there but not the same.

Atlantic Beach is often referred to as The Black Pearl, as it was a Black beach resort for Blacks from the 1930's to the 1970's. Atlantic Beach was born out of segregation, and during that era the wealthy beachfront property owners that came to spend the summers wanted someplace for their servants to go to enjoy the ocean. When I was growing up in the county in the 1950's, Atlantic Beach was a wonderful

Gullah community and the place to be on a hot summer day. It was only a few blocks long, but I have many fond memories of those days at the beach in the ocean on hot days with the mighty waves a-roaring cooling us off. The Atlantic Ocean was still enjoyable and refreshing on our little portion of the beach.

Atlantic Beach is now surrounded on three sides by North Myrtle Beach, and is bordered on the east by the Atlantic Ocean. Atlantic Beach was kind of quasi dormant for decades, and has come back to some extent, but not close to what it was during its glory years. Major developers have acquired some of the land closest to the ocean, and change is a-coming. It is now in the process of being developed by big developers, as there is still a big demand for the oceanfront condominiums.

Progress marches on even when small communities are lost, misplaced or realigned in the process. It is up to this current generation to record and preserve this critical part of our heritage and culture, so that future generations will have a first person account of what it was like in those glory years. Atlantic Beach was alive and bustling in its heyday until the early 1970's. I remember going there in the 1950's and the 1960's.

A major section of the Black community on Myrtle Beach was and still is referred to as The Hill. The night life on The Hill was primarily on Carver Street, and it had most of the little motels, restaurants, night clubs, etc. in its glorious heyday. Carver Street is still a main street on The Hill in Myrtle Beach even today, but it has changed greatly now. The old motels are now closed and most have been demolished. A new generation is on the blocks in the neighborhoods now, and things have changed quite a bit. I often drive through the neighborhoods now just as I did over the decades when I came to visit the area and the old faces and places have faded away and moved on.

A very deep history abounds all over the Carolina Lowcountry, and time has created a natural artistic preservation of many artifacts, old cemeteries, schools, isolated villages, etc. There are a number of heritage sites in many areas and guided tours are available in many instances. Old cemeteries are in the areas, some way back in the woods and off the beaten trails, and some almost lost by time. Some have been destroyed or bulldozed over, as some were in unmarked graves, and there was a lack of records from some of the early years.

A Migration Away and a Remigration Back – We were truly a generation of struggle and the history of the country reflects that for those who care to seek the truth. A generation born into little or no economic opportunities in our home states, and where it took many marches and sit in demonstrations just to obtain certain basic rights in society. Many of us had no choice except to migrate away to get a job and a higher education. Overcoming many obstacles in our journey to survive and return to our roots here by the water's edge.

I constantly roam through many neighborhoods taking in the changes, and even though many neighborhoods are the same as they were decades ago, new generations are residing there along with what's left of the older generation. Many of the younger generation have a different mindset and some are headed in other directions. My old neighborhood has remained virtually unchanged for many decades; some of the same families are still there in the same houses as when I was growing up there in the 1950's. It's the subsequent generations that are the majority there now, in some houses it's the children of the parents who first settled there over a half century ago, and in other houses it's the children and grandchildren.

Gullah History and Culture is Alive and Flourishing Along The Carolina Lowcountry

The Gullah history and culture is still alive and flourishing here along the Carolina Lowcountry and beyond. The countryside and surrounding areas have changed somewhat over time, and different generations primarily stroll here now. All up and down the area you can see the concerted efforts of the people to preserve their culture. Some of the older generation have returned and set up various little shops with artifacts and other cultural items for sale.

The culture passed down from Sea Island slaves on isolated barrier islands still continue to have a very profound effect on their descendants today. Some of their direct descendants still reside on a few of those old isolated islands carrying on in the tradition of their ancestors. They are keenly aware that they are actually living in a perpetual museum. Their homes are now equipped with all the modern conveniences of life, but they remain in physical isolation, especially on isolated islands such as, Sandy Island. The people that reside on these isolated islands today are there because they chose to be there, and will not have it any other way. They have been

Overcoming for centuries. Many generations have lived and strolled here by the water's edge.

The Lowcountry is full of a very deep history of all its' people, and is the home of many cultures. Even in the midst of the many changes and development, it is still apparent that the spirit of the people is to continue working to make it better for all. I wanted to take another stroll by the water's edge just to pause and reflect.

Another Stroll By The Water's Edge

As the sun was setting low beyond the bank of the river, I decided to take another stroll by the Water's Edge just to pause and reflect. It was a serene moment of silence here where so much knowledge and wisdom was passed down from generation to generation. It was as if the old moss laden oak trees were trying to tell me something after all these years. The boats docked there at the landing had motors on them. The years that I remember they only had small rowboats and it took them quite some time to row all the way across the river to get to their little isolated island.

The wisdom by the water's edge that I received so many decades ago is still with me now, even after so many sunsets under the old oak trees. Just as the old man saw his reflection in the last sunset, I looked and saw my reflection in the river as the sun was setting. I took the journey into the deep, deep waters of life and returned safely here because of the knowledge that was passed along to me. I was profoundly prepared and looked forward to Overcoming the obstacles along life's journey. We must all take that journey by the Water's Edge one way or another.

Our past history of overcoming obstacles is a source of strength and inspiration for all people who must struggle through life's treacherous journey. The human Spirit triumphs when a people refuse to give up against all odds.

We have seen much changes over the decades, and especially now in these latter days where so much is happening in the world today. Many people are feeling the stresses and strains of an ever changing global economy with the many uncertainties of today. Many are seeking a change for the better, and some are not sure which way to go and are truly at the crossroads. As I was strolling there by the water's edge I could feel a Change coming; a profound Change Will Come.

As The Sun Sets On The Old Island
You Can Feel A Change Coming

It's Late In The Evening
And A Change Coming

A Change Will Come!
Dark Clouds a-Coming

As I sit on my screened in front porch on a nice Spring day I can enjoy the peace and tranquility here along the Carolina Lowcountry. But as old man wisdom sits under the old oak tree by the water's edge along the banks of the river he can see dark clouds a-coming. A Change Coming! **Daniel** told us about the latter days and a time of great trouble, great trouble! (Daniel 12:1-13).

Jesus gave us the signs of the end in St. Matthew 24:, St. Mark 13:, St. Luke 21: **Jesus said "This generation shall not pass, till all these things be fulfilled"** (St. Matthew 24:34, St. Mark 13:30, St. Luke 21:32). This generation is the fig tree generation (Jeremiah 24). **Jesus said "learn a parable of the fig tree"** (St. Matthew 24:32, St. Mark 13:28, St. Luke21:29-31). This is the fig tree generation; and **"This generation shall not pass, till all these things be fulfilled"**.

Politicians may have a different story, but they haven't put forth a panacea yet. A **Higher Power is in charge!** There is a God in heaven that revealeth secrets to his servants the prophets (Daniel 2:28, Amos 3:7). We can only **reap what we sow** (Galatians 6:7). We need only open our eyes and see who's marching off the deep end into a very painful and prolonged **Economic Stagnation.** There may be some in the Land of Plenty who may think otherwise, but the crisis continues in other areas such as, housing, energy, gas, food, etc., etc. We were told that **Difficult Economic Troubles** would occur (Ezekiel 7:19, Zephaniah 1:14-18, James 5:1-7,

Isaiah 18:1-7). Some will understand and know, and some will not understand (Daniel 12:9-10, Hosea 14:9).

"This generation shall not pass, till all these things be fulfilled". Daniel saw a time of Great Trouble, and we know that **armies will compass Jerusalem** (St. Matthew 24:15, St. Mark 13:14, St. Luke 21:20). The northern armies will be led by Gog (Russia), Persia (Iran), with Ethiopia and Libya marching with them as they **march on Jerusalem.** We know that God will destroy 5/6th of these armies. Zechariah 14:12 tell us what will happen to the people that fought against Jerusalem. We know that the temple will be rebuilt in troublous times (Daniel 9:24-26). **The vile one** will sit in the temple claiming to be God (II Thessalonians 2:3-4, Daniel 8:24-26, 9:24-26, 11:21-25). We know that the major super power of the end time will be the revived Roman Empire, the European Union (EU) as stated in (Daniel 7:7, Revelation 13:1). There may be some in the Land of Plenty and beyond that may not believe; but non belief will not prevent **Bible Prophecies** from **coming to pass. "This generation shall not pass, till all these things be fulfilled".** Behold, we have been foretold all things (St. Mark 13:23).

A **Luciferian Influence** has permeated a large segment of the culture to this day (II Corinthians 11:13-15, St. Mark 7:7, Colossians 2:8, Revelation 12:12). **We are in a spiritual war** (Ephesians 6:11-13, 16-18).

Any nation that forget God shall perish (Deuteronomy 8:19-20). That means you, me, and the Land of Plenty. Repent or perish (St. Luke 13:3, 5). There is only One who can save you (II Peter 2:9, Revelation 3:10, 20). Get renewed in the spirit of your mind (Ephesians 4:23-24, Colossians

3:10). Put on the new man (Colossians 3:10). **"This generation shall not pass, till all these things be fulfilled".**

There really is Only One Way, AMEN! (St. John 10:9, 14:6) Come Now (Isaiah 1:18-20). **A Change Will Come!**

Be Prepared to Compete
In The Global Economic Arena
(And Stay Prepared)

The Global Economic Arena is now before us and The Economic Playing Field has been dictated to us. We must be prepared to Compete in it!

- Identify Potential Job Opportunities (categories) in the Global Economy.
- Identify Economic Skills needed in the Global Economy.
- Acquire Economic Skills (not just degrees) needed in the Global Economy. (Identify your strengths and weaknesses – Reason for leaving last job?)
- Establish Priorities and engage in Economic Networking. (Have Long Term Economic Goals). Avoid that which is Contrary to Sound Doctrine.

- Obtain and Maintain the Proper **A.C.E.** (Attitude – Conduct – Environment).

Attitude	- Must be conducive to Accomplishments.
Conduct	- Don't Engage in Conduct Detrimental to Progress.
Environment	– Avoid Negative Influences and Bad Associations.

Being computer literate is essential for learning and may help you stay ahead of the curve. You can do research online and keep up with the latest technology and financial markets. Information is online. Maintain an up to date resume. You may even have to e-mail your resume.

In every economy in the world there is a need for good financial record keepers, accounting and bookkeeping. Other skills are also needed and in demand, such as, paralegals, medical assistants, auto mechanics, electricians, plumbers, sales, etc.

The economy may be down now with high unemployment, and companies are not hiring. There are many skilled and management people looking for work. Some are even going back to college and making it harder for some first time students to get accepted into college. Colleges and Universities all over the land are receiving more applications than they can accept. Many are becoming discouraged and dropping out of the job market. Different Economic Skills are now needed in the Global Economy.

Don't give up, know who you are, stay committed and prepared. Continue to send out resumes and continue to update and upgrade your Economic Skills. You may take classes at night or online. So be prepared as you may end up starting your own company or business. Continue to turn over dollars in your community as this will help create jobs. Be prepared for your opportunity because in the darkest arena a flickering of light will shine showing you your opportunity. Be Prepared!

Be Prepared! A Change Will Come.
Take The Next Big Step!

The Next Big Step

An Economic Step

The Civil Rights Movement succeeded because it rested on a solid foundation; a deep and abiding faith in God. Major rights, benefits, and goals were achieved by people proceeding in a righteous direction with a movement born in the church. The Civil Rights marchers marched in the streets and endured great sacrifices in order to get justice. There were various sit down demonstrations as well as marches all over the land. Many people sacrificed themselves then so that many rights, benefits and goals were achieved, such as:

The right to equal access in public accommodations, etc.
The right to equal educational opportunities.
The right to equal economic opportunities.
The right to equal voting opportunities, housing, etc.

But rights gained must be exercised-utilized in order to get a benefit from them. We will not continue to receive or get a benefit from such hard fought for rights unless we continue to exercise and utilize such rights. The next step in the Civil Rights Movement must be an Economic Step taken by subsequent generations, so that they can continue to enjoy the benefits their ancestors fought so hard for. This next step must still be anchored on a solid foundation, and a deep and abiding faith in God. We can be the head and not the tail, above and not beneath (Deuteronomy 28:13). Let us get a renewed spirit of the mind, and put on the new man (Ephesians 4:23-24, Colossians 3:10).

A Civil Rights Economic Movement

Civil Rights Economic Movement is needed to continue to receive a utility or Economic Benefit from the Civil Rights gained by the sweat and blood of our ancestors. You cannot fully enjoy your civil rights without having the economic means to do so. We need more Economic Skills. The young generation must take the Next Step, and remain committed and dedicated to acquiring the Economic Skills needed to get a utility or benefit from the rights gained by the Civil Rights Movement.

Our young people now don't have to march in the streets or engage in sit down demonstrations. The young generation of today need only continue to march down the halls of the schools, sit down in the classrooms, and study and work hard to succeed. Just remember the sacrifices so many people made for you so that you can enjoy the benefits you have today. You too can be successful as you now have unlimited educational and economic opportunities. Your goals and objectives can be accomplished as long as you too remain anchored on that same solid foundation, a deep and abiding faith in God. The first step of the Civil Rights Movement succeeded on such a solid foundation and so can this next Economic Step as long as we maintain a deep and abiding faith in God.

The young generation must be prepared to compete in the Global Economy. They will need Economic Skills to compete in the Global Economy. We all need Economic Skills to enjoy the economic benefits and rights gained by the Civil Rights Movement. Just having the right to an equal education will not get you a utility or benefit from such right unless you march down the halls of the schools, sit in the classrooms and study to be successful. You will only reap what you have sown.

We must proceed in a righteous direction. The young generation must take the next big Economic Step while remaining anchored on the same solid foundation that the Civil Rights Movement was anchored on; a deep and abiding faith and belief in God.

It has been over 40 years since the major Civil Rights victories and laws; yet too many of our people are still wandering in the wilderness in this Land of Plenty. We here in this fig tree generation can have the economic victories and the Economic Benefits if we remain connected to our God as we take the next big Economic Step. We have an **Obligation** to those who sacrificed and died in obtaining those rights we now take for granted.

Take The Next Big Step!

A New Beginning can be ours (Isaiah 1:18, Ephesians 4:23-24, Colossians 3:10, St. John 10:9). The Kingdom of God is for all who want it (St. Matthew 6:33, Romans 14:17-18, St. Luke 17:21). We need only come to Jesus (St. Matthew 11:28-30). For there really is Only One Way (St. John 14:6). We can be clean through the word (St. John 15:3). Let us therefore do our whole duty (Ecclesiastes 12:13). Don't remain in the congregation of the dead (Proverbs 21:16). Get wisdom and understanding (Psalm 111:10).

Our sojourn here is not just happenstance; some were chosen before the foundation of the world, by a God that cannot lie! (Ephesians 1:4-11, Titus 1:2, Romans 8:28-33). Remain focused, stay where you are and work to accomplish your Goals and Objectives. Know and fulfill your purpose for being here; know your duty (Ecclesiastes 12:13). You can get a good understanding (Job 28:28, Psalm 111:10). Do not remain in the congregation of the dead (Proverbs 21:16). Our God can prepare a table for you in the presence of your enemies; where your cup runneth over (Psalm 23). Judge not; but every tree is known by his own fruit, good men, evil men, are here. (St. Luke 6:43-46)

Acquire **Economic Skills** and be prepared to compete! Don't be left behind stuck in the mud pile on the bottom of the economic ladder. We have been and are Blessed here in this land, and have been provided everything we need to succeed and be prosperous and healthy. But we must, Study and Work! Study and Work! (II Timothy 2:15, I Thessalonians 4:11, II Thessalonians 3:10-12).

Overcoming
Along The Carolina Lowcountry
and Beyond

Be Prepared to Take The Next Big Step

About The Author

The author was born and raised in a historic old Riverfront Town along the Waccamaw River deep down in the southeast. He is the son of a Gullah chief from Sandy Island, S.C. (his father was the youngest Gullah chief in the history of Annie Village on Sandy Island). He spent many summers on the island as a young child growing up, and his experiences from those years has compelled him to come back to his roots now that he is retired, to record the history of the people and the area as seen from his perspective and vantage point.

He is committed and dedicated to documenting and recording an artistic preservation of the history of a unique people and their culture, through art, writings, books, films, illustrations, etc. A glimpse into the customs habits and folkways of a unique people and their culture.

The author is also an artist and painter, and lived and worked in the San Francisco Bay Area for over 35 years. He also has a degree in accounting from San Francisco State University, and a JD degree from San Francisco Law School. He retired in June 2002 to devote full time to documenting his artistic preservation of, my people down home.

Index

Overcoming

Along The Carolina Lowcountry

And Beyond